1000 Pictures

for Teachers to Copy

Andrew Wright

A copublication of Collins ELT and Addison-Wesley
Publishing Company, World Language Division

Contents and Introduction

Many teachers recognise the usefulness of simple drawings in their teaching. Drawings have many advantages: they are quick to do; their content can be determined exactly by you, the teacher; they are easy to reproduce. But many teachers think they cannot draw! Or if they can draw they feel they have not got enough time.

This book is based on years of enjoyable experience gained in helping teachers to learn how to draw. It contains a careful introduction to drawing and over one thousand drawings for teachers to copy.

Who might use this book?

The main users of this book will be language teachers. However, teachers of other subjects and indeed anyone whose job involves communication will find this material relevant. I have met speech therapists, sociologists, youth leaders, yoga teachers as well as teachers of history, geography and economics who all make use of simple representations.

The organisation of the book and the selection of language items

The sections, topics and language items in this book are based on the *Threshold Level*, a document produced by the Council of Europe for language syllabus designers. I have also referred to the *Cambridge English Lexicon*.

Language is enormously rich. A word can have many meanings depending on context. I have had to be selective and have often only been able to illustrate one of several possible meanings. I have omitted concepts that are impossible to represent pictorially and language items which are relatively infrequent, i.e. within stages 5 or 6 of the *Cambridge English Lexicon*.

Ambiguity

Of course, pictures are ambiguous, thanks to the variety of human minds and experiences. In the early days of audio-visual language teaching, every picture was examined for its ambiguity and all were found 'guilty'. However, there is an increasing awareness today of the way people respond to and interpret information. Above all we realise that objects, actions and words gain meaning through their association with other information. An object in isolation can itself be ambiguous. Is a cow a religious object, a dangerous animal or a source of milk? A word can mean different things according to time, place, cultural context, people concerned and so on. A picture usually contributes to understanding by being a part of a context. It is not surprising that a picture considered in isolation is often found to be ambiguous. See section 6 (pages 119-123). for further discussion on the teaching of meaning through pictures.

Pictorial language

It has often been stated that people who are not familiar with the conventions of pictorial language are unable to interpret a picture adequately. However, it is my contention that these conventions have gained a universality in recent years due to large scale printing and an increased flow of information, making pictures such as the ones in this book more accessible worldwide.

Are simple drawings insensitive and a threat to artistic vision?

Teachers of art and others concerned with the development of their students' artistic vision are often critical of teachers who make use of crude symbols. However, the fault lies, not in the notion of simple drawings, but in the use of crude generalisations and clichés . . . and these can also be found in speech. I hope you will feel that the majority of ideas given for drawing in this book are not based on a closed system but on the development of a sensitive awareness of forms in life.

Using pictures in language teaching

Traditionally, pictures have been used for description or for illustrating a recorded dialogue. In recent years, however, there has been an emphasis on the communicative use of language. Pictures are very useful in this respect. They provide references to which the learner can make a personal response, such as expressing likes or dislikes.

Group work is essential if communicative competence is the aim. There is no alternative if each learner is to have the opportunity to try to use the language he or she has learned. Pictures provide a focus for this essential activity.

This is only a brief look at the role of pictures in language teaching. Further ideas for using pictures are given in Section 6.

1 How to draw

In the first section I have reproduced the way in which I help people to draw more effectively. The level is higher than you need for copying the drawings in this book. However, I have decided to put it at the beginning of the book because you need basic help even for copying.

Essentially, in order to copy (i.e. without photocopying!) you must:
1 judge proportions (is a line is longer or shorter than another, or a shape thicker or thinner);
2 judge the angle of the lines (whether they are lines or the edges of shapes).

These are the main things. However, it will also help you to study how I draw solid people. When you learn my approach you will be able to copy my solid people much more easily. Similarly with the settings: when you learn how I have avoided using perspective, you will be able to copy them much more easily.

So, please, even if you are only going to copy the pictures in this book (and not produce your own), do look through this first section. Thanks.

Materials and techniques

Card or paper

Teachers' flash cards should certainly be on card and not paper. Card lasts longer and is easier to handle. For pupils it may be as cheap to use duplicated sheets rather than card. In Britain it is possible to get cheap or free offcuts of paper and card from printing houses.

Adhesives

Sometimes you may want to stick thin paper to card. You can:
1 use a rubber based glue which does not wrinkle the paper. Professional designers do this.
2 use a paste. If you use a paste put it on the thin paper and leave the paper to expand for some time before putting it onto the card.

Photocopying

1 Don't go to the edge of your paper.
2 Don't use larger areas of black than your machine can reproduce.
3 If you stick smaller pieces of paper down so that the levels are different put typist's white opaque along the edges to remove the shadowed line.

Grids

To give a sense of organisation to your text and pictures arrange them within a frame and align their edges. A frame (in British English – a 'grid') may be made of one, two or even more columns.

Tracing

If your top piece of paper is too thick for you to see the image clearly put them both against a window pane and copy it like that.

How big?

Letters should be about two cms high. But guiding rules like this are not very useful. Try a sample – see what it looks like from the back of the class.

Colour

It is so tempting to use lots of bright colours in order to please the students. Much better to choose colours for other purposes:
1 to make an object more recognisable if the shape is rather ordinary, for example, an orange;
2 to direct attention to something, particularly if it is small within a picture, for example, one person giving another a present. The people could be drawn in black line and the present in a colour;
3 expressive or decorative reasons for using colour are probably less important for the language teacher making his/her own pictures.

How to draw
stickpeople

— no necks, no shoulders

— no hips, no hands

COPY THE DRAWINGS BUT NOT TOO SMALL.

Amazing facts about the human body
The head and body are equal in length to the length of the legs.
The arms are as long as the body.

A TIP Don't bother with hands unless you want him to hold something or point...

More amazing facts

elbows are halfway down the arms and point backwards

knees are halfway down the legs and point forwards

I don't like these stickmen.

Make the lines straight and make them meet.

The flicky style is distracting and even hard to 'read' especially if there is a background.

How to draw
stickpeople

We can only interpret a stickman's actions if he has the essential features of a 'real' person: so you must copy real people's actions. Don't try to draw from memory until you are more confident.

The 'real' people you must copy could be you (yourself, acting out the position and copying each bit, starting with the body) or a friend or someone in a photo.

TIP If you or your friend are acting out a position, then close the curtains and lock the door in case you are looked upon and judged crazy!

Here are some actions to copy. Study the *angles* of the body, then the arms and legs. Judge the angles of each bit by comparing it with either a vertical or a horizonal line.

You can only see one arm.

Note the very narrow angles between the legs and between the arms and the body.

Note the key points in slow running: the arm is bent and at right angles and the foot is well off the ground.

How to draw
stickpeople

Copy these drawings. Start with the body.

Start with the chair, then do the body.

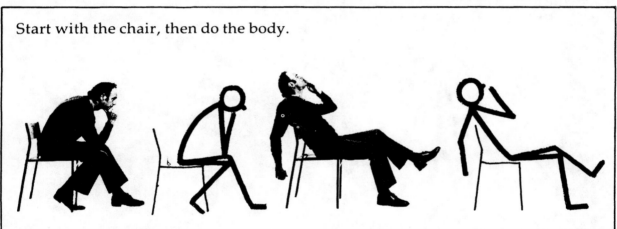

Make drawings from these photographs, stick by stick. Start with the body.
Compare the angles with vertical and horizontal lines.

How to draw
stickpeople

Characters

Note: noses show which way the person is looking.

Balance

This ballet dancer is falling over because her weight is not over her foot.

He can't pick up the box because his foot is not beneath his weight

✓   ✗   ✓   ✗

Draw furniture, cycles *first*.

Two thicknesses of line (and/or colour) make the drawing less confusing.

How to draw
boxpeople

Box people are useful because they have character and can be seen more easily than stick people in a complicated picture.

The vital action of the boxman is achieved exactly like that of a stickman. However, start with the body.
What sort of body do you want to give him?
Choose one!

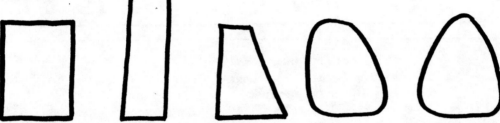

Draw the body first. Then draw stickmen limbs in the action you want. Draw the limbs from the corners of the box.

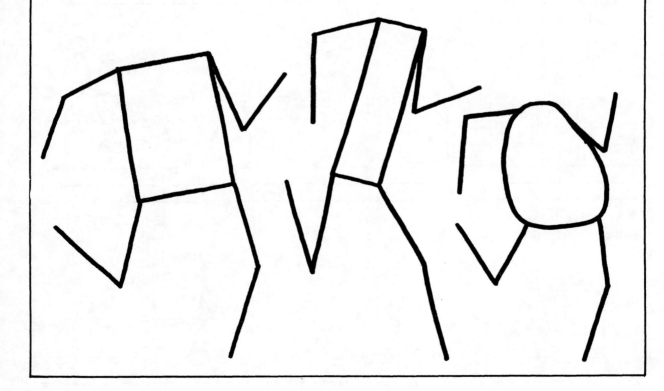

How to draw
boxpeople

Now draw in lines representing the other side of the limbs.
These lines should not imitate subtle folds of cloth etc.

Draw in the feet as triangles. Don't try to represent real shoes;
it is too difficult and not worth the effort.

Draw in the heads and hands.

Now the patterns, tones and textures can go in.

How to draw
boxpeople

Here are some more boxmen all drawn in the same stages as outlined above. Note how lines 'disappear' behind bodies or other limbs.

Most of the drawings in this book are of stickpeople because they are fast to do. However you can make any of them solid by the technique given here.

How to draw
faces

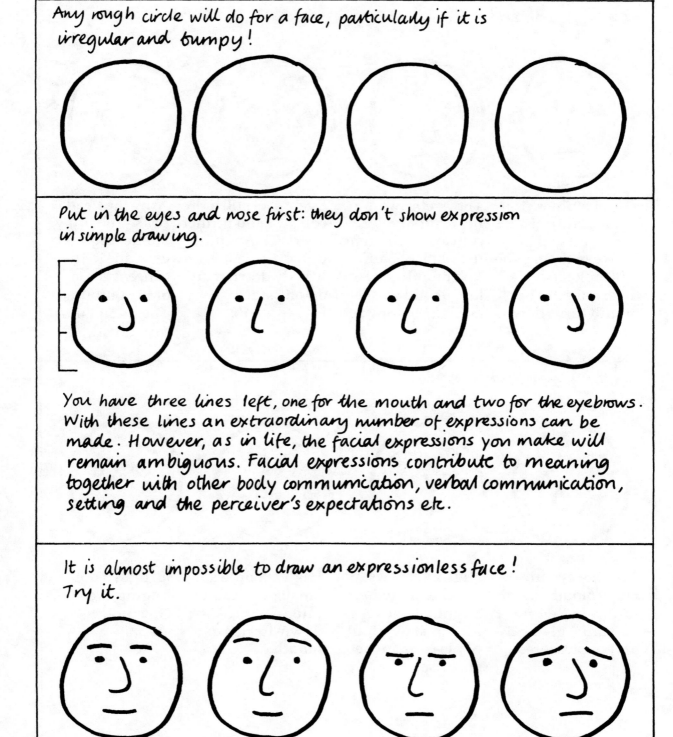

Any rough circle will do for a face, particularly if it is irregular and bumpy!

Put in the eyes and nose first: they don't show expression in simple drawing.

You have three lines left, one for the mouth and two for the eyebrows. With these lines an extraordinary number of expressions can be made. However, as in life, the facial expressions you make will remain ambiguous. Facial expressions contribute to meaning together with other body communication, verbal communication, setting and the perceiver's expectations etc.

It is almost impossible to draw an expressionless face! Try it.

High eyebrows show surprise.

Low eyebrows show concentration.

Angled eyebrows show pain.

How to draw
faces

Getting sadder !

The eyebrows rise in the centre. There must be a gap between them or he will look too determined. The mouth turns down.

The eyebrows are now slightly concave – this gives that look of pain. The mouth is now longer and weaker and further down.

Eyebrows still more concave and further apart. The mouth, down-turned, is weakly down more on one side.

Now the head is back. The brows are nearer the eyes due to the concentration of the outburst. The mouth must turn down.

Getting more surprised !

Arching eyebrows. Small mouth, in this case very slightly upwards, giving a hint of pleasure.

High eyebrows, not too close together. Slightly larger eyes. Mouth shows hint of pleasure in the surprise.

High eyebrows. Small eyes, rather intense. Small down-turned mouth.

Surprised horror. Bulging eyes. Tiny mouth.

How to draw
faces

Getting happier all the time !

The eyebrows rise and curve.
The mouth begins to curve upwards.

The eyebrows are not only high and rounded but are now further apart. The mouth, of course, is now a fuller smile.

The distance between the eyebrows is so important for that simple open smile.

Now the head goes back (you show this by placing all the features higher on the face). The eyes close. The mouth opens.

Getting grimmer !

This face is surprised, almost sad! The eyebrows are rather high. The mouth looks a little weak – perhaps because it is rather low.

The eyebrows are now nearer to the eyes and nearer to the centre. The mouth is bunched and a little nearer the nose.

The eyebrows now touch the eyes. They nearly meet *and* they tip downwards towards the centre.

One eyebrow rests on the eye: the other has flown upwards. There is a compressed fold of skin between the eyebrows. Note the corner of the mouth is *down*.

How to draw
faces

Here are more faces showing how the positions and shape of the three lines can produce many expressions. Note the combination of angry eyebrows with a smiling mouth.

Note: in younger people the features are lower down the face.

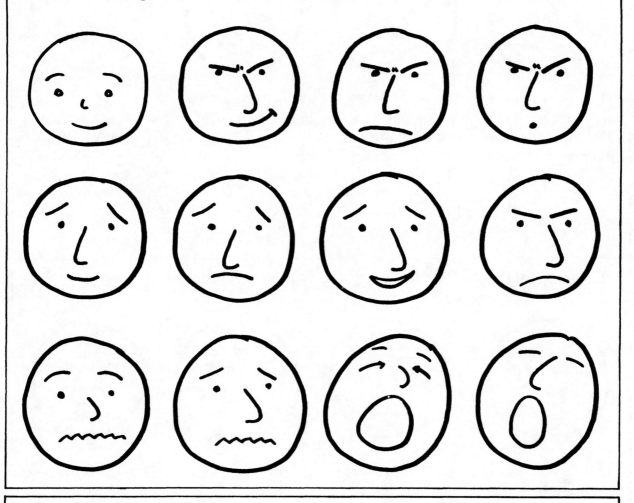

Plus a few more lines!

How to draw
faces

How to make more individual faces

Hair, different eyes, clothes, make all the difference!

How to draw
caricatures

Essentially caricature means exaggeration.
If someone has a squarish head it is made square. If he has a longish pointed nose it is drawn very long and very pointed.
Position of features: if the eyes are near the top of the head they are drawn *at* the top of the head.

A real test of a caricature is if you can redraw it from memory. For people with poor visual memories this means being able to remember the appearance of the caricature in words.

Try it with the caricatures drawn above. Look at them for a few moments, describe them to yourself, and then, remembering this verbal description, try to draw them from memory.

How to draw
caricatures

Make use of shapes you can give a word to:
they are easier to remember.

Build up your caricatures out of these bits.

How to draw
caricatures

pear head
eyebrows small and at top of head
eyes big and dark

nose begins at top of head
and echoes shape of head

mouth small

pear body smaller than head
stick arms

legs a little longer than head
legs close together

small triangular feet

walking sitting/eating cycling running picking

seeing ghosts pointing carrying sitting lying in bed

How to draw
caricatures

a lucky charm.
He wears it at all times,
even in bed.

short hair; he rejects the
long hair style.

big ears and eyes; he likes to
know everything that is happening.

sly smile
big chin; he likes to think he
looks tough.

pointing; he likes
telling people
what to do.

money, but not too much;
he is saving his money to buy
a fast car.

large boots; he is rather rough
with other people and his boots
symbolise this characteristic.

Having invented a caricature like this, ask the students
to suggest the kind of characteristics given here.

To show he can do things

playing   riding a motorcycle   drinking

How to draw
caricatures

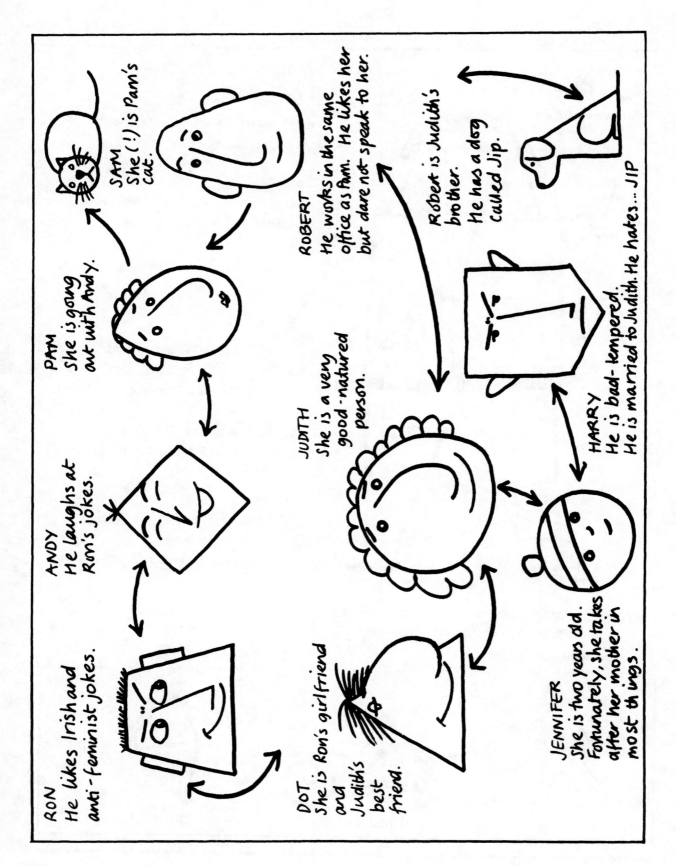

SAM
She (!) is Pam's
cat.

PAM
She is going
out with Andy.

ANDY
He laughs at
Ron's jokes.

RON
He likes Irish and
anti-feminist jokes.

DOT
She is Ron's girlfriend
and
Judith's
best
friend.

JUDITH
She is a very
good-natured
person.

ROBERT
He works in the same
office as Pam. He likes her
but dare not speak to her.

Robert is Judith's
brother.
He has a dog
called Jip.

HARRY
He is bad-tempered.
He is married to Judith. He hates... JIP

JENNIFER
She is two years old.
Fortunately, she takes
after her mother in
most things.

How to draw
caricatures

How to draw
caricatures

How to draw
caricatures

How to draw
animals and objects

If you want to draw from a real object or a
photograph of it, there are, basically, two
things to think of: first of all, the
proportions of the basic shape(s) and
secondly the angles of the edges of the
shape.

Basic shape of objects

If you want to make a drawing of a car, first of all fit it
into a very basic shape like a rectangle. Get the rectangle correct!
Is it too fat? Make it slimmer! Is it too slim? Make it fatter!
These are the only two questions to answer at this stage.

Angles of the edges of the shape

When you have got the proportion of the main rectangle correct,
look for important internal shapes and get the angles correct.

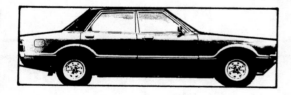 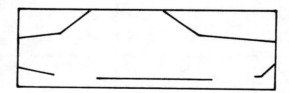

Now you have got the main proportions and shapes correct
you can add the few essential details which will confirm to the
viewer that it _is_ a car.

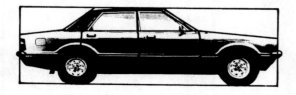 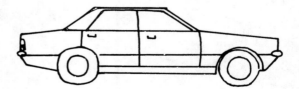

How to draw
animals and objects

Exactly the same approach can be applied to any objective
drawing you do.

the box can
be removed
and a few
curves put in.

How to draw
animals and objects

Here are more examples of how to find basic shapes in a variety of creatures.

Once you have this basic shape you can put in a few important curves and details.

Note: I prefer to find a rectangle as a basic shape.
It is much easier to judge the proportions of a rectangle or a triangle than a circle or oval.

Try to find a rectangle for this sheep!

How to draw
animals and objects

There are many animals and objects drawn in this book which you may wish to copy.

On these two pages (pages 27-28) you will see how I made the final drawings and how you can copy them.

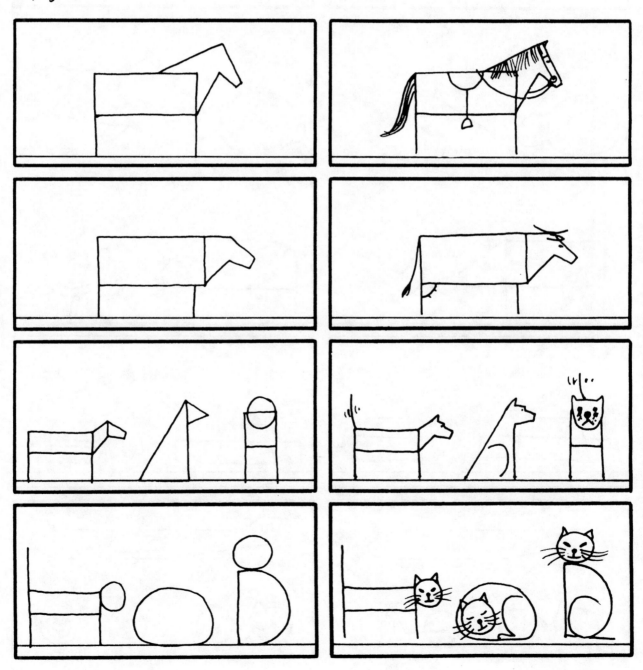

How to draw
animals and objects

How to draw
scenes and objects
and avoid perspective

The idea of concentrating on basic shapes and their proportions together with the angles of the main sides can be used for anything. You do not need to know about perspective if you can copy shapes and angles!

Note the angle of the pavement with the vertical side of the picture.

Although the first aim of this book is to give you drawings to copy, you will still need these basic approaches to get your copying right.

How to draw
scenes and objects
and avoid perspective

Avoid all perspective drawing if at all possible. Draw buildings and similar objects face-on rather than going away from you. It is nearly always possible! Compare the drawings below. On the left are some typical attempts to draw perspective. On the right is the easy and effective solution.

On the right nearly all the lines of the furniture and the buildings are either vertical or horizontal. Also note that the chairs, the table and the people's feet are on the ground line.

Here are two more. There are many more in the section on **settings.**

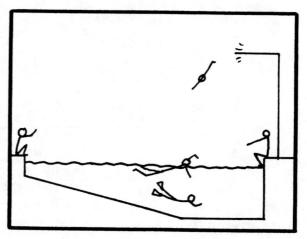

How to draw
scenes and objects

Of course, when you draw something 'flat on', without perspective, you must still make decisions. You must decide which view to take. Some objects are easier to recognise from the front, some from the side.

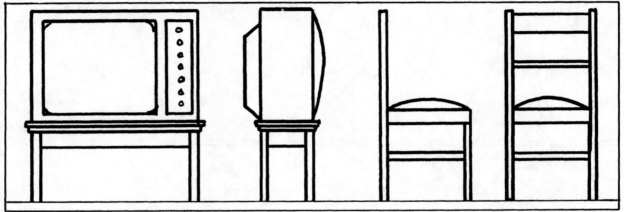

Televisions are most easily recognised from the front.

Chairs are most easily recognised from the side.

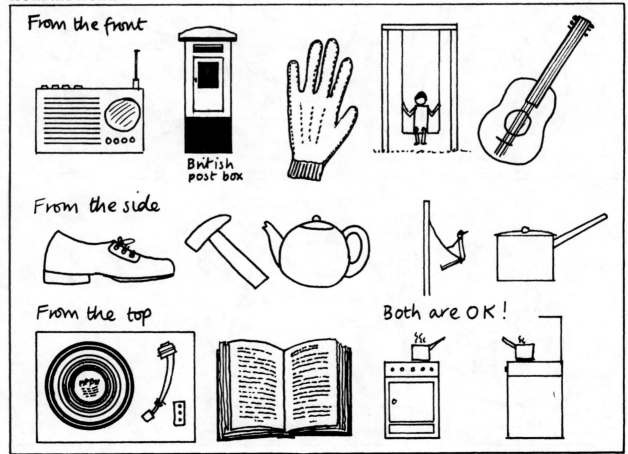

From the front

British post box

From the side

From the top

Both are OK!

How to draw
special effects

shaking

KNOCKING

knocking

dizzy

anxious

pain

heat

steam

heat

How to draw
special effects

How to draw
Materials and techniques

Thick and thin
Two thicknesses of line used on the same artwork look very effective. On the blackboard you can use the point of the chalk and the side of it, e.g. note the thin box and the thick lines of text and drawing.

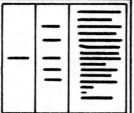

Gestalt perception
Some of the principles of gestalt are useful to the designer. The idea of grouping information so that it has an obvious connection is seen on this page.

Big and small
Any contrast of shapes gives a stimulating effect.

Similarity and proximity
Similarity of shape, of tone, of colour or of size all suggest a connection.

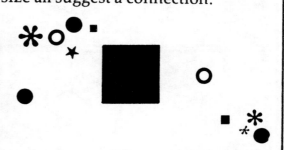

Square and round
Contrast of roundness and of squareness and of angularity are attractive because of their variety.

Regularity and irregularity
Irregular shapes contrast with regular shapes in an attractive way.

Dark and light
A line may not be bold enough by itself. Filled in shapes have strength by their contrast with background.
It helps to group the information (gestalt).

2 Settings

When people say they cannot draw they often mean they cannot draw things in perspective. In fact, perspective (in the sense of parallel lines converging to a vanishing point) is usually unnecessary! Indeed, it is often clearer *not* to use perspective and it is certainly much faster. On page 36 I have drawn one of the pictures of the street in perspective in order to demonstrate that there is no particular gain.

If you draw flatly across the picture all the lines on buildings will be either vertical or horizontal. But avoid perspective even in the case of objects like cars or even a brush! (See pages 29-30).

Thick and thin lines

In a scene there are a lot of lines: this can be confusing for the student. Of course, you can use colour to identify one subject from another. If you cannot use colour, as I cannot in this book, you must use different thicknesses of line. For example, draw all the stickpeople with a thick line and the background with a thin line.

Another way of separating people away from the background is to draw them as solid people or boxmen. In the following section I have used both stickpeople and boxpeople to show what the effect looks like.

Lines which are sketchy and which do not join up with other lines of the same object also cause confusion.

All these points relate to the 'gestalt' theory of visual perception, which argues that we gather together visual information we think belongs together.

For uses of settings by language teachers, see Section 6, pages 119-123

Street

Park and garden

Terrace and countryside

Beach and mountains

Bus station and bus

Train and aeroplane

To be effective this drawing must fill the blackboard!

Kitchen and bathroom

Settings
Dining room

Sitting room and bedroom

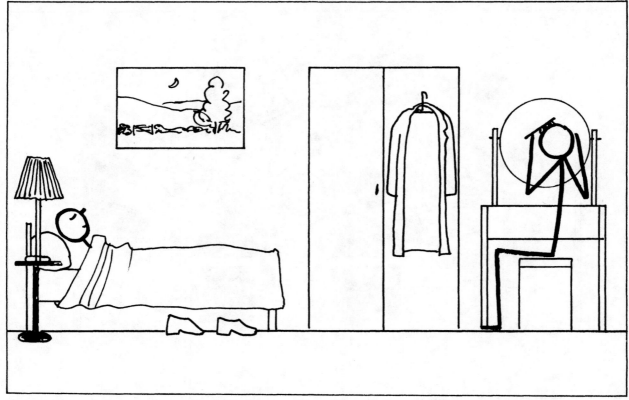

Settings
Baker and supermarket

Restaurant and café

Travel agent and hotel

Settings
Post office and telephone booth

Settings

Hospital and doctor's waiting room

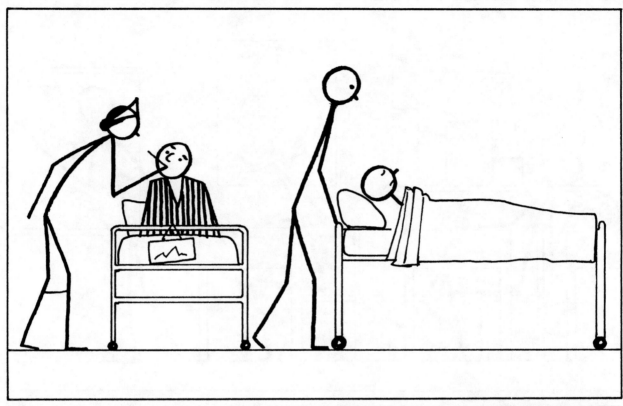

Classroom and police station

Library and museum

Art gallery and cinema

3 Topics, behaviour, notions

How to draw

In order to copy these drawings you will have to make judgements about angles and proportions. Have you looked at Section 1 How to draw?

Subjects covered

The subjects are taken from the Council of Europe *Threshold Level* contents list. I have omitted Education – you will find some pictorial reference in Section 2. Household articles are under 'House and home'.

Ambiguity

These pictures are not expected to illustrate unambiguously the word you are trying to teach (see introduction).

Personal identification
(appearance)

note: the head is large in comparison with older people. young (child)	young (adult)	middle aged	old
note: the features are lower down and the chin is small young (child)	note: plenty of hair and careful look. young (adult)	note: less hair, slight frown and plump chin. middle aged	note: thin hair, hollow cheeks, lines. old
note: small head for scale tall	short	fat	thin
strong	weak	broad-faced	thin-faced
dark-haired	fair-haired	bald	curly-haired

Personal identification
(appearance)

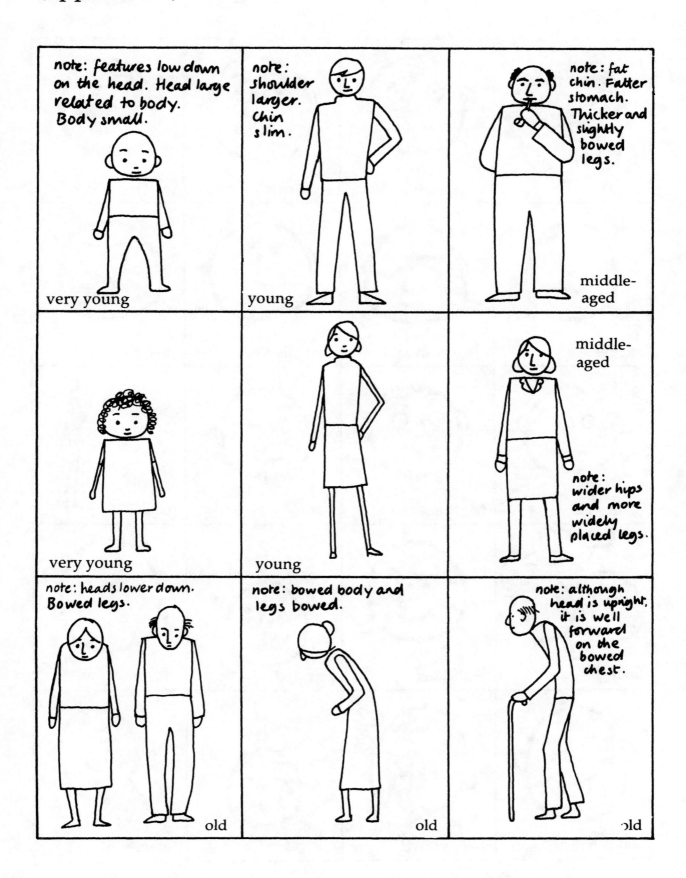

Personal identification
(moods and emotions)

angry

bemused

contented

curious

depressed

determined

disbelieving

disgusted

dismayed

frightened

happy

irritated

loving

malicious

puzzled

sad/unhappy

self-satisfied

sleepy/tired

surprised

thoughtful

Personal identification
(family relationships)

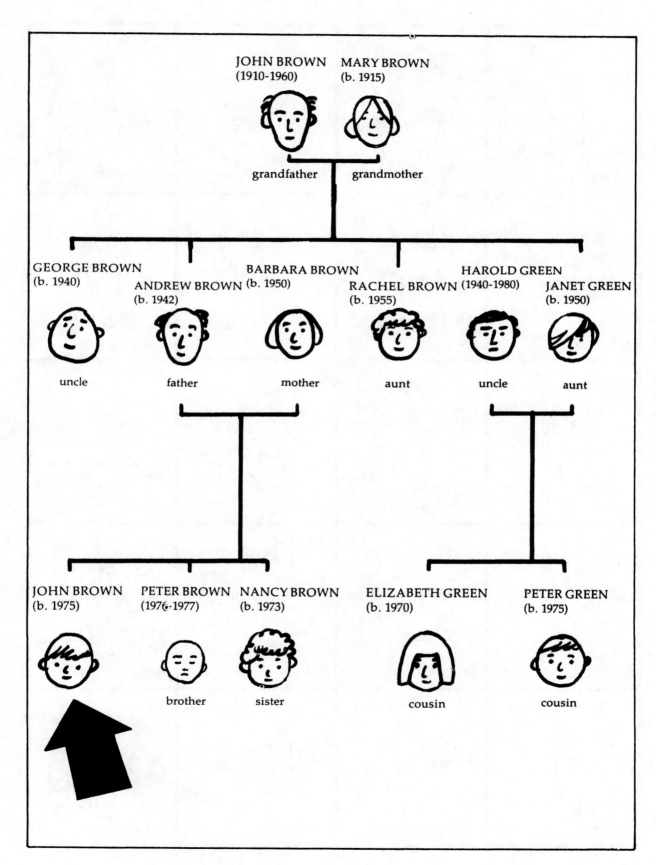

Personal identification
(professions/occupations)

architect	artist	baker	businessman/woman
butcher	chemist	cook	doctor
driver	factory worker	farmer	fireman
footballer	greengrocer	grocer	joiner
labourer	mechanic	milkman	miner

Personal identification
(professions/occupations)

musician

nurse

office worker

photographer

pianist

pilot

policeman

policewoman

postman

shop assistant

soldier

seaman

street cleaner

teacher

typist

unemployed

waiter

writer

yoga teacher

Topics, behaviour, notions
House and home
(rooms etc.)

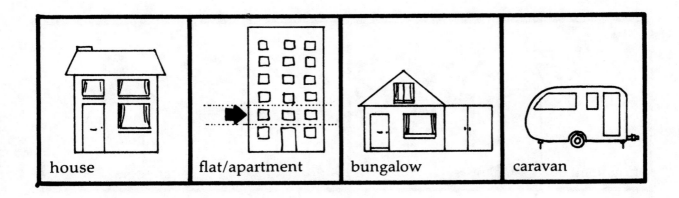

house | flat/apartment | bungalow | caravan

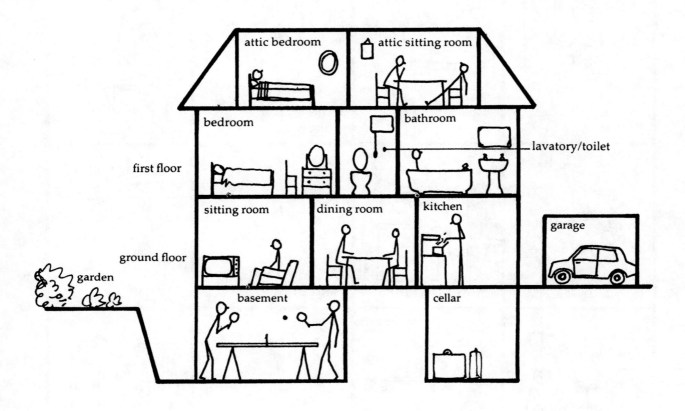

attic bedroom | attic sitting room
bedroom | bathroom
lavatory/toilet
first floor
sitting room | dining room | kitchen
garage
garden
ground floor
basement | cellar

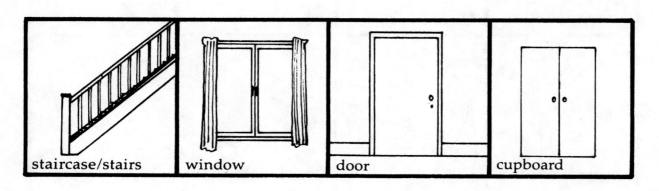

staircase/stairs | window | door | cupboard

House and home
(furniture and amenities)

armchair

bath

bed

blanket

bookshelves

chair

chest of drawers

clock

coathooks

computer

cooker

cupboard

desk

dishwasher

dressing table

hand basin

hot and cold water

lamp

mirror

picture

House and home
(furniture and amenities)

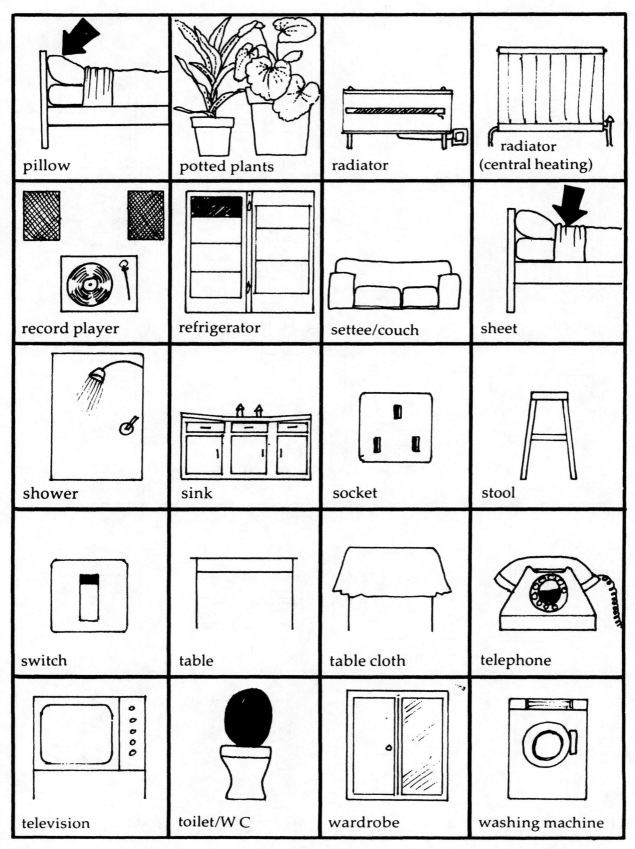

pillow	potted plants	radiator	radiator (central heating)
record player	refrigerator	settee/couch	sheet
shower	sink	socket	stool
switch	table	table cloth	telephone
television	toilet/W C	wardrobe	washing machine

House and home
(household articles and tools)

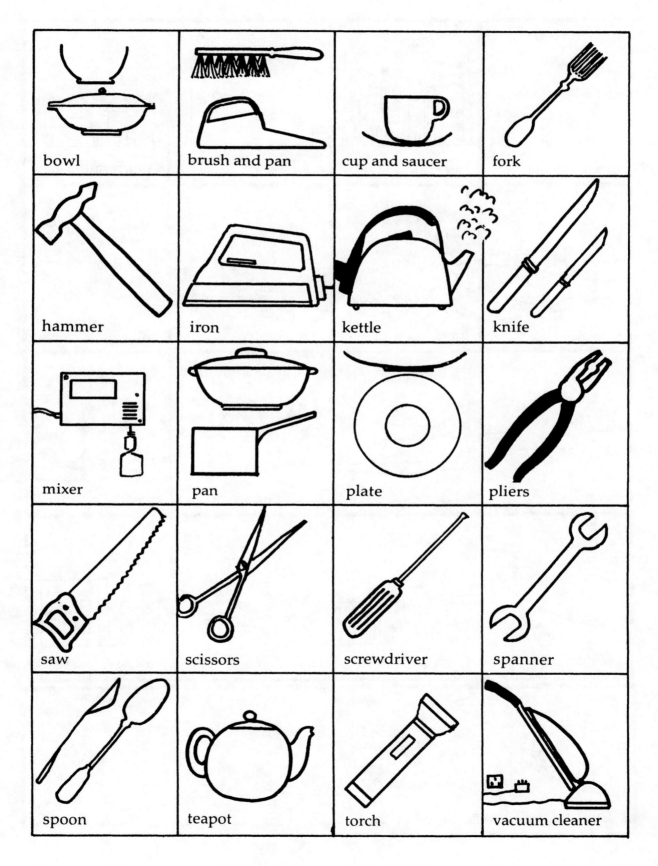

bowl	brush and pan	cup and saucer	fork
hammer	iron	kettle	knife
mixer	pan	plate	pliers
saw	scissors	screwdriver	spanner
spoon	teapot	torch	vacuum cleaner

Topics, behaviour, notions
Regions

canal

city

factory/ industrial area

farm/farming area

fields

forest

flat country

hill

island

lake

mountain

river

seaside

town

valley

village

Topics, behaviour, notions
Animals

bat	bear	bee	bird
bird	butterfly	camel	cat
cat	cock(erel)	cow	crab
crocodile		deer	dog
dog	elephant	fish	frog

Topics, behaviour, notions
Animals

giraffe	goat	goose	hedgehog
hen/chick	horse	kangaroo	lion
monkey	mouse	owl	pig
rabbit	shark	sheep	snake
swan	tiger	tortoise	whale

Topics, behaviour, notions
Plants

branch	cedar	fir	oak
palm	poplar	root	trunk
bush	cactus	corn	grass
hedge	leaf	marsh	seed
chrysanthemum	daffodil	rose	tulip

Free time and entertainment

acting

ballet (going to)

baseball

basketball

bird watching

camping

car racing (watching)

chess (playing)

cinema (going to)

clothes (making)

collecting (stamps)

computer (playing computer games)

concerts (going to)

cooking

cricket (playing)

cycling

dancing

disco-dancing

driving

Free time and entertainment

fencing	films (watching)	fishing	football
gardening	hang gliding	hiking	hockey
javelin (throwing)	jogging	jumping	model making
movies (going to)	opera (going to the)	painting	pets (looking after)
photography	picnics (going on/having)		poetry (writing)

Free time and entertainment

radio (listening to)

reading

records (listening to)

riding

rock climbing

running

sailing

shopping

singing

skiing

snorkelling

squash (playing)

sunbathing

swimming

table tennis

television (watching)

tennis (playing)

theatre (going to)

touring

video (making)

video (watching)

walking

water skiing

yoga

Travel and places
(types of transport)

by bicycle	by boat	by bus	by camel
by car	by elephant	on/by foot	on horseback
by hovercraft	by lorry/wagon	by motorcycle	by scooter
by plane	by roller skates	by ship	by taxi
by train	by underground		by unicycle

Travel and places
(road features)

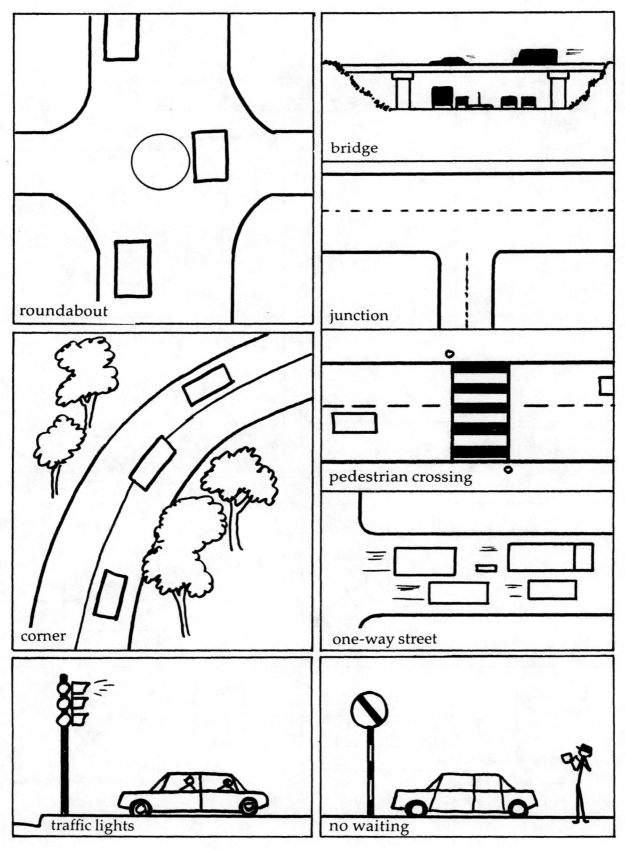

roundabout

bridge

junction

corner

pedestrian crossing

one-way street

traffic lights

no waiting

Relations
(invitations and correspondence)

dinner

tea

coffee

party

cocktail party

bring a bottle party

would you like a drink?

present/gift (giving a)

writing a letter

receiving a letter

telephoning

friends

not friends

lovers

Health and welfare
(parts of the body)

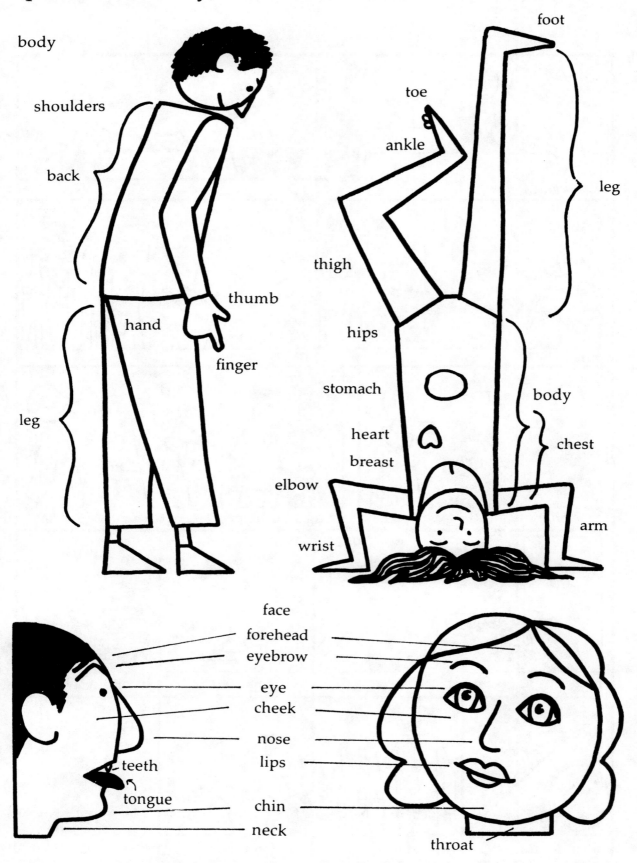

body

shoulders

back

thumb

hand

finger

leg

foot

toe

ankle

leg

thigh

hips

stomach

body

heart

chest

breast

elbow

arm

wrist

face

forehead

eyebrow

eye

cheek

nose

lips

teeth

tongue

chin

neck

throat

Health and welfare
(ailments, accidents, medical services)

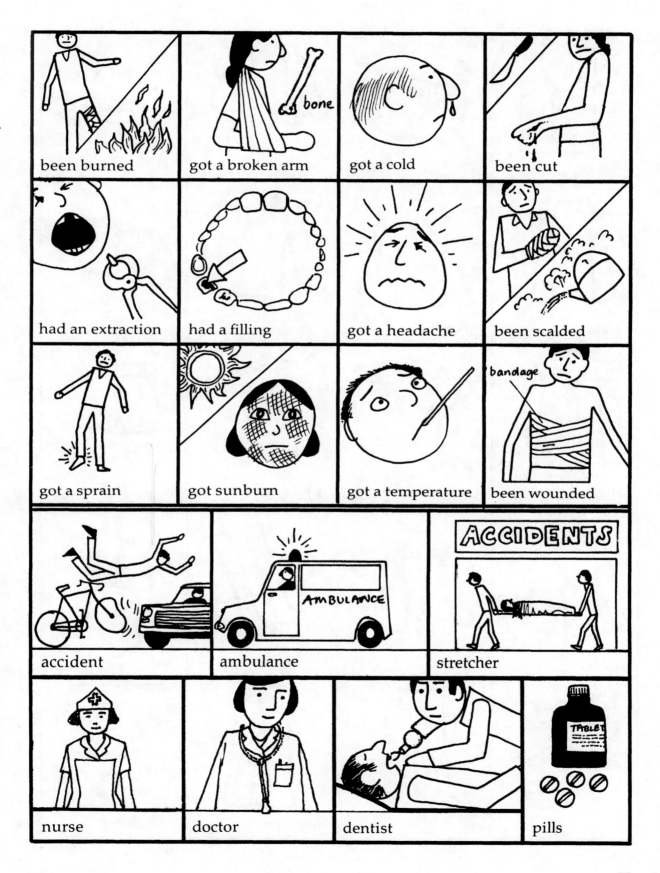

been burned

got a broken arm — bone

got a cold

been cut

had an extraction

had a filling

got a headache

been scalded

got a sprain

got sunburn

got a temperature

been wounded — bandage

accident

ambulance — AMBULANCE

ACCIDENTS

stretcher

nurse

doctor

dentist

pills — TABLET

Clothes

blouse	cap	coat	hat
jacket	jersey	pullover	purse
raincoat	scarf	shoes	shorts/belt
skirt	socks	stockings	suit
suit	tights	trousers	underwear

Topics, behaviour, notions
Food and drink

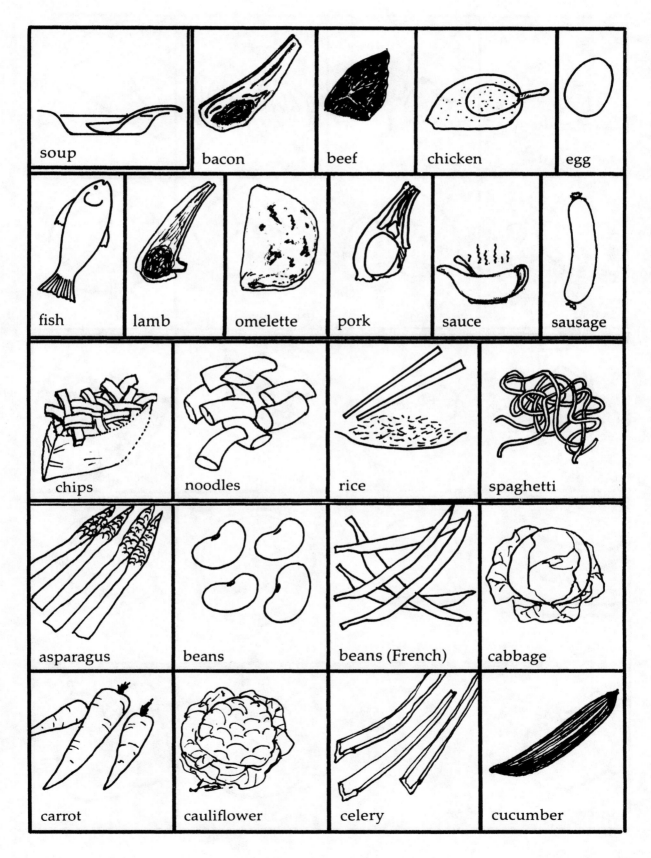

soup bacon beef chicken egg

fish lamb omelette pork sauce sausage

chips noodles rice spaghetti

asparagus beans beans (French) cabbage

carrot cauliflower celery cucumber

Food and drink

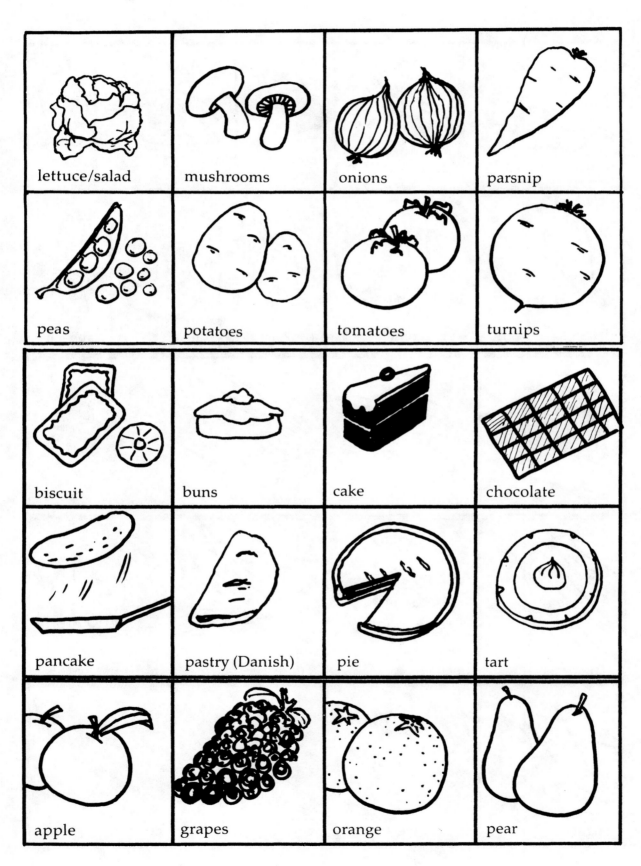

lettuce/salad	mushrooms	onions	parsnip
peas	potatoes	tomatoes	turnips
biscuit	buns	cake	chocolate
pancake	pastry (Danish)	pie	tart
apple	grapes	orange	pear

Topics, behaviour, notions
Food and drink

raspberries

strawberry

cheese

cake

beer

coffee

cream

juice

milk

mineral water

tea

water

wine

bread

sandwich

barbecue

boil

fry

grill

roast

Weather

sun	moon	star	sun shining
overcast	storm	thunderstorm	lightning
raining	windy	snow	ice
fog	very cold	very hot	I'm hot
I'm cold	I'm wet	umbrella	wellington boots

4 Illustrated vocabulary and grammar

In Section 4 there are over 500 drawings illustrating prepositions, verbs, passives, adjectives and nouns. In some cases you could copy the drawing onto the blackboard and use it to teach the meaning of the associated word. (See 'Teaching meaning with pictures' p 117). In other cases the picture is best used to contribute to an overall experience which helps the student appreciate the meaning of the associated language.

These drawings are more useful for practice than for presentation. The drawings can be used to cue alternatives in sentence patterns, or to cue answers to questions or as reference and the starting point for discussion, conversation and stories. (See 'Some basic ways of using pictures in language teaching', pages 119-123).

Illustrated vocabulary and grammar
Prepositions

about (the room)

above

across

after

against

go along the path

among

at

before

behind

below

beneath

between

by

down

for

from/to

in

inside

into

Prepositions

near (the cathedral)

next

on

onto

out of

outside

over

past

round (the moon)

through

to

under

up

with (a broken handle)

come with us

without

Verbs

Illustrated vocabulary and grammar
Verbs

bring

build

burn

buy

call

carry

catch

catch

choose

clean

climb

close

come (on)

come (down)

cook

copy

count

cough

crawl

cry

Verbs

cross	cut	dance	dance
demand	deny	descend	dig
disagree	disappear	dive	divide
draw	dress	drink	drive
drip	eat	enter	examine

Illustrated vocabulary and grammar
Verbs

fail

fall

fall off

fetch

fight

fill

finish

fire

float

fly

follow

frighten

gather

get (wet)

get/receive

get (down)

get (in)

get (on)

get (on)

get (up)

give   grow   guide   hang

help   hide   hit   hitch-hike

hold   hunt   imitate   improve

insult   introduce   invite   jog

join   jump   keep (quiet) keep

Verbs

kick	kiss	kneel	knock
laugh	lean	learn	leave
lend	lie	lift	light
like	live	listen	listen (to)
lock	look	look (after)	look (at)

Verbs

look for	lose	love	make
marry	meet	mend	mix
move	obey	offer	open
pack	paint	part	pass
pass	pay	pick	pick (up)

Verbs

play	point	polish	post
pour	prefer	pull	push
put (down)	put (away)	put (on)	quarrel
raise	read	receive	refuse
remain	remind	repair	rest

Verbs

return	ride	ride	rise
run	sail	save	search
seize	sell	send	serve
shake	share	shave	shout
show	shut	sing	sit

Verbs

skate	sleep	slide	slip
smell	smile	speak	spill
splash	stand	stand (up)	start
stay	stamp	sting	stir
stroke	study	support	sweep

Verbs

take

take

take

take (off)

talk

taste

telephone

tell

thank

think

throw

tie

touch

try

turn

turn (on)

turn (off)

visit

wait

walk

Illustrated vocabulary and grammar
Verbs

wash	watch	wave	wear
win	wipe	wish	work
worry	wrap	write	yawn

Passives

She's having her photo taken.

They're having their house painted.

It's eleven o'clock. She wants to go to bed: the cat has been put out. The garage has been locked. The lights have been switched off. The radiator has been turned off. The washing up has been done.

being posted

being collected

being taken

being sorted

VICTORIA

being taken

being put on

being taken by

being taken off

POST OFFICE

being taken to

being sorted again

being delivered

Illustrated vocabulary and grammar
Adjectives

absent

afraid

aggressive

alive

alone

ancient

apart

asleep

bad

bald

bare

beautiful

big

blind

blond(e)

bloody

blunt

brave

bright

Illustrated vocabulary and grammar
Adjectives

broad	busy	calm	careful
careless	cautious	cheap	cheerful
clean	clear	clever	close
cloudy	cold	comfortable	content
cool	correct	costly	crooked

Adjectives

crushed	curious	dangerous	dark
dead	deaf	dear	deep
delicate	delighted	different	dirty
dry	easy	eldest	electric
empty	endless	enormous	equal

Adjectives

expensive	false	fast	fat
favourite	first	flat	fond
forgetful	formal	fresh	full
funny	generous	gentle	greedy
half	happy	heavy	helpful

Adjectives

high	hollow	honest	hot
huge	humorous	ill	important
impossible	inside	instant	intelligent
jealous	kind	large	last
late	left	light	little

Adjectives

lonely

long

loose

loud

middle

middle-aged

narrow

nervous

new

next

noisy

old

open

opposite

painful

polite

powerful

precious

proud

Adjectives

quiet	rainy	rapid	respectful
responsible	rich	right	right
ripe	risky	rough	round
rude	rusty	sad	selfish
serious	shallow	sharp	short

Illustrated vocabulary
Adjectives

shy	sick	silly	similar
skilful	sleepy	slow	small
smooth	snowy	sore	stormy
straight	strict	strong	sunny
tall	tame	tense	thick

Illustrated vocabulary
Adjectives

thin	thirsty	thoughtful	tiny
unconscious	unhappy	untidy	unwilling
useful	violent	weak	wealthy
wet	wicked	wide	wild
wise	woollen	wrong	young

Illustrated vocabulary
Nouns

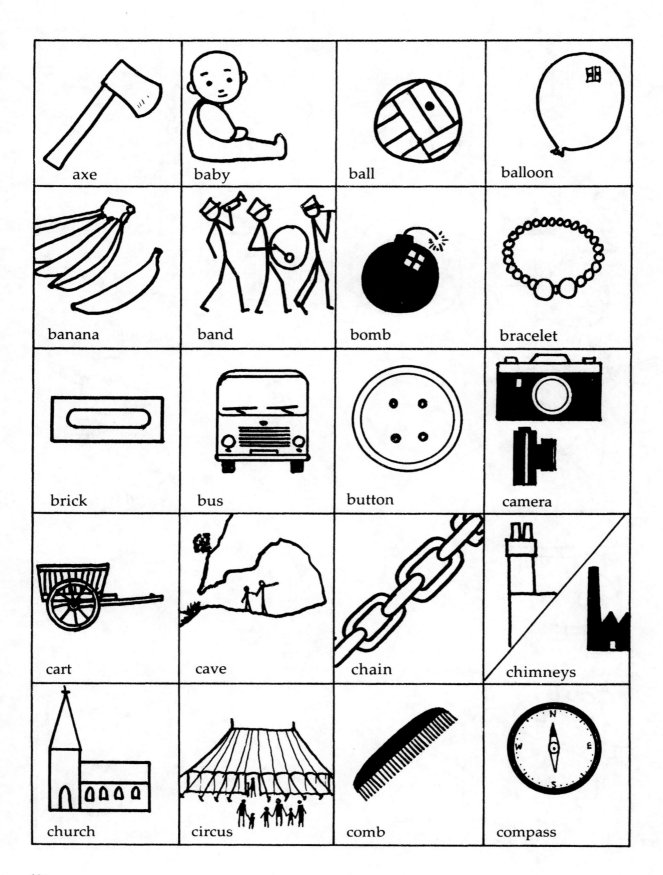

axe	baby	ball	balloon
banana	band	bomb	bracelet
brick	bus	button	camera
cart	cave	chain	chimneys
church	circus	comb	compass

Illustrated vocabulary and grammar
Nouns

cork	crowd	curtain	cushion
devil	doll	drum	dustman
earring	envelope	family	feather
fire	fireplace	fist	flag
flame	freezer	gate	guitar

Nouns

hairdrier	handbag	handkerchief	handles
ice cream	ink	jail	jar
jug	key	king	kite
knot	lift/elevator	lipstick	loaf
lock	luggage	matches (box of)	microphone

Illustrated vocabulary and grammar
Nouns

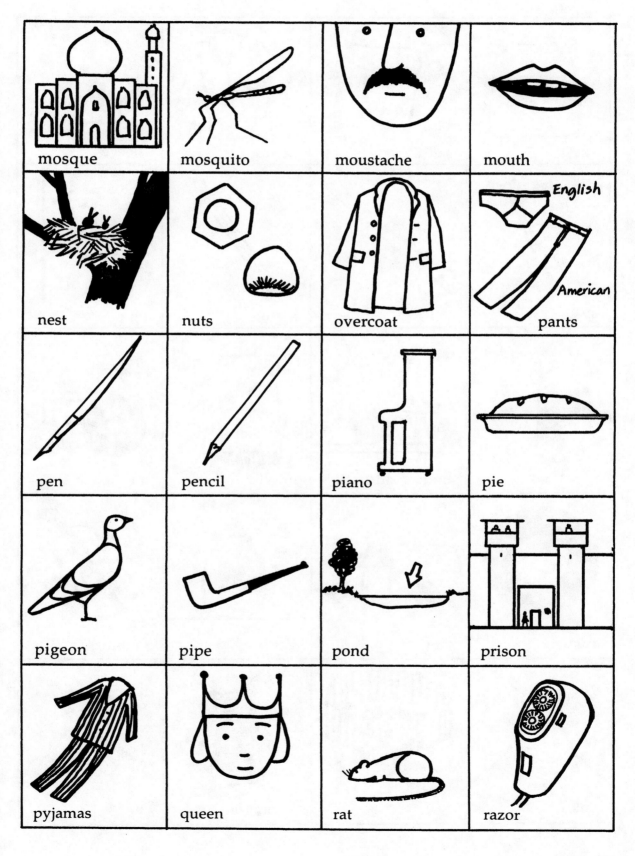

mosque	mosquito	moustache	mouth
nest	nuts	overcoat	pants
pen	pencil	piano	pie
pigeon	pipe	pond	prison
pyjamas	queen	rat	razor

Nouns

sack	saddle	shirt	sleeve
spade	stick	sword	tap
tie	toothbrush/paste	towel	tractor
tyre	van	vase	violin
volcano	watch	windmill	zip

5 Pictures for Composition

It is quite easy to invent speculative pictures and story sequences. However, people do not usually think it is going to be easy so they do not even try. When you have copied some of these you will feel more confident in doing your own.

Individual speculative pictures

The secret of inventing these is to clear your mind of any specific incident. The picture must be ambiguous! For ways of using these pictures, see page 122.

Story sequences

Once more I think it is better to allow a certain ambiguity in the story. Fairy stories and other traditional tales give a clear story to illustrate, see 'Beauty and the Beast', page 116.

For ways of using these pictures, see page 121.

Individual speculative pictures

Pictures for composition
Individual speculative pictures

Story sequences

Pictures for composition
Story sequences

Story sequences

Teaching meaning with pictures

Using one picture

happy   man   walking   reading   tree

Usually a single picture is too ambiguous to teach the meaning of a new item. It might be enough to teach 'tree' with a single picture.

Using several pictures

They are reading.

They are working.   *Several examples help to direct the learner's attention to the aspect in common to all.*

Contrasting pictures

man   woman   girl

happy   unhappy

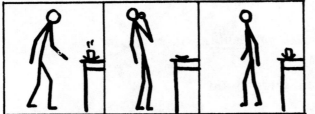

He is going to drink his tea.

He is drinking his tea.

He has drunk his tea.

It is sometimes easier to teach contrasting concepts rather than one by itself.

Comparing pictures

run

sprint

Fine comparisons rather than broad contrasts are essential for some concepts.

Sequence pictures

The idea of 'running back' is only understandable if one knows where he has come from.

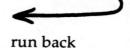

run back

Cause and effect

He was sick because he ate some bad mushrooms.

He caught cold because he got wet.

The idea of something happening due to __another__ happening needs a combination of drawings.

Some concepts can only be perceived and understood within a sequence of events.

6 Some basic ways of using pictures in language teaching

I hope that people with concerns very different from those of language teachers will find this book useful as a source of pictures. However, language teachers and in particular teachers of foreign or second languages will probably be the chief users and it is for them that I am adding this section.

It is not possible in the space available to describe the nature of language teaching aims and methods, for example contrasting recent movements towards communicative competence with the more traditional emphasis given to formal accuracy. I have concentrated, therefore, on listing basic ways in which pictures might be used and not on evaluating these uses in terms of learning outcome.

The methods and the roles of visual materials in listening and reading activities as well as in speaking and writing have many similarities. Partly for this reason and partly due to the need for brevity I am discussing these four activities under two headings rather than four. There are a number of recent books rich in suggestions for using pictures in language teaching at all levesl; reference is made to these in each of the following sections.

Listening and reading

Some roles for visual materials

1 To interest the student
2 To help to 'translate' the meaning of the gist of the text or of individual items of language
3 To give a context for the language and student activity
4 To give cultural information
5 To contribute to the search for specific information in the text and to help the student demonstrate non-verbally that s/he has found that information and understood it.

A single picture may be used to teach the meaning of a word or phrase new to the student. However, pictures are usually ambiguous: people interpret them differently.

The most useful contribution a picture can make is to contribute to the student's understanding of a more general context which may be made up of pictures, the teacher's actions, sound effects and words. And it is in the understanding of this overall context that the language new to the student will have meaning.

There is another way of thinking about the role of pictures. It is normally assumed that the picture is supposed to *illustrate* the new meaning. And this is one way of using pictures (see the two previous pages).

However, sometimes it is the *way* the picture is used and referred to which gives meaning to the 'new' language. The most obvious example is to put away a picture and then to challenge the students' ability to remember it. This immediately calls for the use of a past tense form. (For example, show a picture of an action or actions and, putting it away, ask, 'What was he doing?' Thus the past tense form is illustrated not by the picture but by the way in which the picture has been used and referred to.)

The *way* in which pictures can be used to promote language which is not actually illustrated in the picture is discussed at length in a number of books: see McAlpin, J., *The Magazine Picture Library*, and Maley and Duff, *Drama Techniques in Language Learning*. (See section on Further reading). This exploitation of the picture has great significance in *all* areas of language learning.

Demonstrating understanding

Essentially, all the techniques listed here involve the student in matching information in the text, heard or read, with non-verbal information in the picture.

Texts describing people, places, objects, etc.

A number of pictures are shown to the student and s/he must point to, tick, number, colour or complete the drawing of the appropriate picture according to the text.

The text may be the simple naming of objects or actions or the qualities of them or their position. Longer texts in which there is deliberately distracting information can be used with some advanced students.

A simple way of following up this idea would be to photocopy a page of, for example, objects from the book (removing the text), give each student a copy and then describe each object or its use out of order. The students would simply number the pictures in the order you described them. (Alternatively, a page of characters, pages 20-23).

Bingo is a game based on the same basic idea. Each student has a set of pictures. Pictures are named or described by the teacher. When the student hears one of his/her own pictures named he crosses it out. The first student to cross out all his/her pictures calls 'Bingo' and has won the game.

Alternatively, the students might have a copy of a composite picture (a scene with various people in it, see pages 36-52). They then tick or encircle and number the order in which these features of the picture are described.

Dialogues

Pictures of people talking, either separate pictures or in a composite scene are shown to the students. A conversation is played on the tape recorder or reproduced in written form and the student indicates which people are speaking. (You might use some of the scenes pages 36-52, the pages of characters, pages 20-23, on the people on pages 54-55).

Sequences

A number of pictures presented out of sequence are studied by the students. After listening to or reading a text these are then numbered or arranged in the appropriate order.

Story sequences are the most relevant for this purpose but lists of objects or actions can also be represented in this way. Sequences or arrangements of objects and people in a setting can also be represented on the magnet board, flannelboard, blackboard or OHP. The magnet board is particularly useful for this purpose as figures can be added, moved or taken away with such ease. (See pages 114-116).

Writing and speaking as a demonstration of comprehension

By studying selected pictures a student can complete gapped sentences, choose and write out multiple-choice answers or simply answer questions in which the content of the answer is to be found by studying the picture(s) given. These are the more traditional tasks set for demonstrating comprehension and associated with testing.

Speaking and writing

Some roles for visual materials

1 To motivate the student to want to speak or write
2 To create a context within which his/her response will have meaning
3 To provide the student with information to use in controlled practice work. Pictures showing objects, actions, events and relationships can cue answers to questions, substitutions and sentence completions.
4 To guide spoken and written descriptions or narrations or dialogues
5 To promote discussion and to provide reference

Pictures providing information for answers

The simplest way of using a picture is to ask a question about it. The answer may be a single word or may require the student to structure a sentence and thereby test and give practice in the use of structures and tenses. The information represented in the pictures can be used to cue answers to the questions, to cue substitution of vocabulary items or the completion of sentences. This may be done orally or in writing and is a well-established use of pictures.

The pictures may all be seen together on a chart, blackboard, OHP or on a student sheet. Alternatively, separate pictures may be placed face down and thus not seen, but be picked up and seen for the first time. They can then be picked up and used as the information is required.

This is preferable as it contributes interest and, more importantly, contributes a reason for speaking if no-one except the speaker can see the picture.
For example:
A pile of pictures showing foods, placed face down.

Student A (picking up a picture), Do you like pears?
Student B Yes./No./Sometimes.
Very much. They're delicious.
I can't stand them!

For more example of this use of pictures see Kerr, J.Y.K., *Picture Cue Cards for Oral Language Practice*, and Buckby and Wright, *Flash Cards*.

There are a number of interesting variants on

these well-known ways of using pictures for controlled practice.

Spot the difference

Two or three pictures which are the same except for a number of details are examined by the students. Each difference is described. The differences can be designed so that the sentences used to describe them can be of the same construction; for example, 'In the first picture the cat's tail is longer than in the second picture. In the first picture the table is higher than in the second picture.'

Technically, such drawings are relatively easy to produce. Make a photocopy of your first drawing (one of the settings from pages 36-52). Then, on the photocopy, white out the details you wish to omit or to change.

Memory

Various memory games involve the student in making use of a fixed sentence pattern. For example, fifteen pictures of men and women, each with an identifying feature are placed face down. One student picks up a picture. The other tries to remember what that card was. If s/he is right s/he is given it, otherwise it is replaced.
'Is it the woman with the cat?'
'Is it the man with the hat?'
'Is it the boy with the curly hair?

For more 'game-like' controlled practice activities, see various games books:
Wright, Betteridge and Buckby, *Games for Language Learning*,
Lee, W.R., *Language Teaching Games and Contests*, Buckby and Wright, *Flashcards*.

Pictures as cues in dialogues

Pictures can be used to cue substitutions within dialogues in which the basic sentence patterns are determined by the teacher. Such dialogue work, after an initial demonstration, would normally be done in pair or group work. The pictures would either be printed on a single sheet and taken in turn or each picture would be on a single piece of paper or card and turned over or taken by a student. The advantage of the latter lies partly in the element of surprise and interest; more importantly, however, the advantage lies in the creation of an 'information gap' between the students. If only student B sees the picture there is some reason for student A asking the question. The importance of 'information gap' and 'opinion gap' to language

learning is discussed fully elsewhere. (Johnson, K., *Communicative Syllabus Design and Methodology*, McAlpin, J. *The Magazine Picture Library*, to name two of the many sources.)

Any pictures of single objects or actions may be used. For a wealth of ideas for using pictures for the practice of structures and tenses, see Heaton, B., *Practice through Pictures*. For ideas for using pictures for more functional orientated exchanges see, Kerr, J.Y.K., *Picture Cue Cards for Oral Language Practice*. For ideas for the use of pictures in practice generally, see Byrne, D., *Teaching Oral English*, Wright A., *Visual Materials for the Language Teacher*, Buckby and Wright, *Flash Cards*, McAlpin, J., *The Magazine Picture Library*.

Pictures as cues for guiding written composition

There are several basic ways of using pictures in order to guide written composition.

A written text with gaps may be given to the student and a picture or pictures provide the source of information for completing the gaps.

Alternatively, the text is given in jumbled order. By reading the different sentences and studying the pictures the student is able to rewrite the text in sequence.

A composite picture or a sequence of pictures is necessary for this activity. (See pages 114-116).

Pictures as a stimulus for spoken and written composition

Written composition

A single picture or sequence of pictures without textual guidance is the traditional test in written composition. This established use of pictures need not be described further.

A variation which provides for more interest and is quite easy for the teacher to organise is as follows: show the first picture by itself and ask the students to start writing a story based on it. After five minutes ask them to read what they have written to their neighbour. You might ask one student to read out his version to the whole group. Then show another picture which may not have any obvious relationship with the previous one. Tell the students they must continue their story without any break. Continue in this way with three or four pictures.

Other well known techniques include showing a sequence with one picture missing. The students write the story and are expected to guess at the content of the missing picture.

Speaking

A single picture for interpretation:

A reasonable development of conversation between the teacher and students would be broadly as follows:

Description

First of all, the students should describe in very simple terms what they can see. What can you see in the picture? How many people are there? What's this? etc.

Interpretation

Very quickly individual interpretations of what is represented become apparent and should be encouraged as they lead to genuine exchanges of views. It is advisable for the teacher him/herself not to allow anyone's interpretation to 'crush' another's. For example, experience using this picture shows that people imagine the scene is inside a house, others believe it takes place outside a house.
What is happening? (What do you think? Do you agree?)
What has happened? What will happen next?
Why do you think it is a house/hut/factory/school/, etc?
Why do you think it is a back door and not a front door?

Personal experiences

Such an incident can naturally lead to the question 'Have you ever broken a window?' Students will usually be quite keen to tell you. To release the flood of stories you could ask them to tell their neighbour of their experiences. And you might, finally, invite students to tell the rest of the class about their neighbour's 'doings'.

Broader issues

Very often a broader issue can be discerned and highlighted by the teacher. For example, the question of punishment, initially for the breaking of windows but finally the role of punishment in society.
Do you think that was fair? What do you think should happen? What is punishment for, do you think?

Written and acted conversations

Ask the students to imagine a conversation between the people (or other people not depicted, e.g. a neighbour) before, during or after the incident depicted. They should write the conversation down, perhaps with another student, and then act or read it out.

A sequence of pictures

If there is a degree of ambiguity in the pictures, all the better! The ambiguity provides a reason for speaking. The students might discuss the sequence in pairs, evolving their story and writing it down. The stories may then be read aloud to the class and the differences discussed, particularly in so far as they derive from a literal interpretation of the pictures.

Other ways of using the sequence

Dialogues may be written and acted out; the story may be written from the viewpoint of one of the participants; an interview on behalf of a newspaper can be carried out and an article written; a related social or philosophical issue might be discussed; a simulation might be played out.
For some of these in practice refer to Fletcher and Birt, *Newsflash*.

Media

Blackboard

Whenever possible do your drawings on paper/card or on OHP transparencies so that you can use them again. (Preparing pictures at home also means you can draw in peace and produce them the instant you need them.)

If you do wish to draw on the blackboard it is of tremendous help if you have at least tried out the drawing beforehand, perhaps copying it from this book or from a photograph.

Many teachers say that the very inadequacy of their drawings catches the students' attention. However, even a good joke begins to lose its attraction when relentlessly repeated! Professional illustrators would find it difficult to draw any action or animal or object on the board if they had not previously studied it. So, if you find it difficult to draw on the board without some preparation you are quite normal!

One way of retaining interest and class discipline while you draw is to ask the students to guess what you are drawing.

Growing, changing drawings are possible on the blackboard: they are not possible when pre-prepared. This factor plus the interest on seeing something being made is the blackboard's great strength. (See Mugglestone, P., *Planning and Using the Blackboard*.)

Magnet board/flannel board

In recent years a new substance rather like plasticine has in many ways overtaken both these media in convenience. Small balls of the substance on the back of a piece of paper can stick to most surfaces. Drawings or magazine pictures can thus be instantly displayed and moved about. Solid people rather than stick-people are essential. People, animals and objects can be stuck and moved around on a setting, providing reference for the practice of specific language items or for less controlled composition or a support for listening comprehension.
(See Byrne, D., *Using the Magnet Board*.)

Wall pictures

The scenes in this book will prove invaluable here. A composite picture, as Donn Byrne has shown (Byrne, D., *Wall Pictures for Language Practice* and *Teaching Oral English*) can provide information cues in controlled practice as well as a stimulus and reference for composition.

As with all pictures it is essential that the vital details are big enough and clear enough. Solid figures would normally be clearer than stick figures in a wall picture.

Picture cards for class use: flashcards

Such cards must be one of the most flexible of the media – particularly now that Bluetack and its equivalents allow the teacher to stick the cards on to the board or on to cupboards, etc. Their chief role is in intense oral work both controlled and open. The ease with which a picture can be produced, shown to the class or to an individual and then put away helps the teacher to create a sense of urgency and drama.

A picture card can, of course, simply cue a response as described above. However, there are more game-like activities with cards in which 'information gaps' or 'opinion gaps' can be created thus giving a reason for speaking.

For example, a series of action cards are shown to the students. When they are familiar with the ones in your hand (about six or seven of them) show one card to *half* the class (group A). Then tell everyone to concentrate and feel the telepathic waves! Group B then has three guesses: 'Is he swimming? Is he jumping? Is he

playing football?' See if telepathy works: try the experiment twenty times and record each time a group guesses correctly within three guesses. This simple sentence pattern is an intrinsic part of the activity. Furthermore, it is used as a genuine question. The students really want to know. Even a drill can be communicative!

Here is another example of the use of a picture card, in this case for open unguided communication; take any picture card showing a few objects or people on it. Hold it so that the class see the reverse side of the card, then spin it very rapidly! They will only see a flash of the picture and will protest! However, experience of playing this game shows that people *do* see something. Gradually, as you spin the card again and encourage discussion the picture is established. For many more ideas on the use of the picture card, see Buckby and Wright, *Flash Cards*.

Picture cards for group use

The cards can obviously be smaller than for class use. Their main purpose is to cue language in controlled practice. A single sentence pattern or a mini-dialogue is set by the teacher and written on the board or on a piece of card which all the group can see. The picture cards are usually placed face down. When it is a student's turn to speak, s/he picks up a card and refers to it in his sentence.
For example, pictures of foods:
Student A (picking up a card), Do you like (chips)?
Student B Yes, I do./No, I don't.
Yes, I love them./No, I hate them.
There are many examples of the use of picture cards in Kerr, J.Y.K., *Picture Cue Cards for Oral Language Practice*, or Buckby and Wright, *Flash Cards*.

The overhead projector

Pictures can be shown on the OHP with ease. They can be prepared beforehand, produced at the right moment, moved around on the screen, have text added to them and then be stored away to be used again . . . and again. Such is the flexibility of the OHP in terms of the way in which pictures and text can be used that all the skills at all levels can be catered for.
For ideas on the use of the OHP, see Jones, R, *The Overhead Projector*.

Further reading

Aytoun and Morgan *Photographic Slides in Language Teaching* George Allen and Unwin
Byrne D. (ed) *Communication Games* British Council
Byrne D. *Interaction Packages* Modern English Publications (Sets of materials for group work, about £5 each)
Byrne D. *Progressive Picture Composition* Longman
Byrne D. *Using the Magnet Board* George Allen and Unwin
Byrne D. *Teaching Oral English* Longman
Byrne D. *Wall Pictures for Language Practice* Longman (TB, PB and wallpictures, about £15)
Byrne and Wright *Say What You Think* Longman
Byrne and Wright *What Do You Think, Books 1 and 2* Longman
Buckby and Wright *Flash Cards* Modern English Publications (80 flashcards and TB, about £6)
Candlin C.N. (ed) *The Communicative Teaching of English* Longman
Davies and Whitney *Reasons for Reading* Heinemann
Dakin J. *The Language Laboratory and Language Learning* Longman
Fletcher and Birt *Newsflash* Edward Arnold
Geddes and Sturtridge *Listening Links* Heinemann
Granger C. *Play Games With English* Heinemann
Heaton B. *Practice Through Pictures* Longman
Hill and Mallet *Teaching With Cartoons* Oxford University Press
Holden S. (ed) *Visual Aids for Classroom Interaction* Modern English Publications
Johnson F. *Stick Figure Drawing for Language Teachers* Ginn
Johnson K. *Communicative Syllabus Design and Methodology* Pergamon
Jones R. *The Overhead Projector* George Allen and Unwin

Kerr J.Y.K. *Picture Cue Cards for Oral Language Practice* Evans (TB and 300 picturecards, about £32)
Maley and Duff *Drama Techniques in Language Learning* Cambridge University Press
Maley, Duff and Grellet *The Mind's Eye* Cambridge University Press
McAlpin J. *The Magazine Picture Library* George Allen and Unwin
Mugglestone P. *Planning and Using the Blackboard* George Allen and Unwin
Romo and Brinson *Visual Delights* Mary Glasgow Publications
Wright A. *Visual Materials for the Language Teacher* Longman
Wright, Betteridge and Buckby *Games for Language Learning* Cambridge University Press

Modern English Teacher, Modern English Publications, PO Box 129, Oxford OX2 8JU
Practical English Teaching, Mary Glasgow Publications, 140 Kensington Church Street, London W8 4BN

Source of the topics and language in this book:

Hindmarsh R. *Cambridge English Lexicon* Cambridge University Press
Oxford-Duden *Pictorial Dictionary* Oxford University Press
Trim J.L.M. (et al) *Systems Development in Adult Language Learning* Pergamon
Van E.K. and Alexander *Threshold Level English* Pergamon
Van E.K. and Alexander *Waystage English* Pergamon

Index

A copublication of Collins ELT and Addison-Wesley
Publishing Company, World Language Division

© Andrew Wright 1984

First published 1984
Reprinted 1985

This edition for the USA and Canada
first published 1985

For sale only in the USA and Canada

ISBN 0-201-09132-1

18 19 20-CRW-04 03 02 01 00

Illustrations by the author
Photographs by Robin Lord ABIPP